this is OUR YEAR

Not everyone gets a second chance - but we have! Let's live life to the fullest + enjoy every step of the way - together! I love you Patrick Sally Jami Yami Pittburgh Goldman loves me!

Constantly yours,
Julie Ashley
Call me

Dedicated to Maag Maag & Gaga

This is Our Year by Lien Design, Inc.
San Diego, California 92013

how to
USE THIS BOOK

In this day and age, it's harder than ever to find time to connect and bond with your significant other. This journal is a fun and easy way to take a break and spend a few minutes reconnecting and exploring each other's worlds.

We know you'll find so much joy discussing these questions that you may even wind up doing 2 or 3 in a row over a good bottle of ~~wine~~ *Sparkeling water*, or while watching the ~~sunset~~ *Snow fall* together.

Each question has space below it where you can jot down notes if desired. Those spaces were intentionally made small because this notebook is more about having a conversation than it is about keeping track of your answers.

There's no wrong way to use this journal. It was designed to be used once a day. But don't be hard on yourselves if you miss a day here and there. The important thing is that when you do find those moments to connect, you'll have this enjoyable tool to spark up new conversations that may surprise you!

DAY 1 ✔

What could someone do for you that would make you really happy?

Jö suitcase $$$ + fast/luxurious car. For me(P) to stay sober + healthy

P: find passion → purpose for my life

DAY 2 ✔

If you could be world-famous for one thing, what would it be and why?

J: Motivational speaking / Singer (kid)
↳ slash writer/producer/
entrepreneur/
business-
woman

P: Improve the quality
of as many peoples' lives
as possible / Athlete (kid)

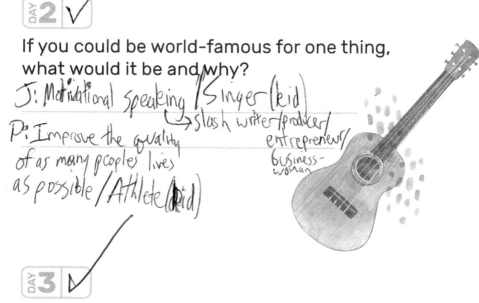

DAY 3 ✔

Do you like public displays of affection? Where do you draw the line?

J: Yes, around business

P: Yes, except around family

DAY 4 ✓

If you could travel back in time and change how you handled one thing in your life, what would it be?

P: Don't do drugs

J: Pick up the phone (Gate)

DAY 5 ✓

If you were offered 20 million dollars to leave the country and never contact your family again, would you take it?

J: Hell Yes!

P: No

Swiss Chalet

DAY 6 ✓

How would you describe your ideal romantic date?

J: Patrick - not rushed, alone time, making love

P: Julie - no phones, some itinerary w/wiggle room (cum together)

What do you think is your strongest selling point in your job?

P: punctuality, care, energy/initiation, problemsolving,
J: level of expertise, ability to motivate, passion, vision, unconventional thinking
persistence

What do you think is the secret behind couples that have lasted over 30 years?

J: Fulfilling others needs, trust & beliefs in other's words
needs.

P: renewal of love

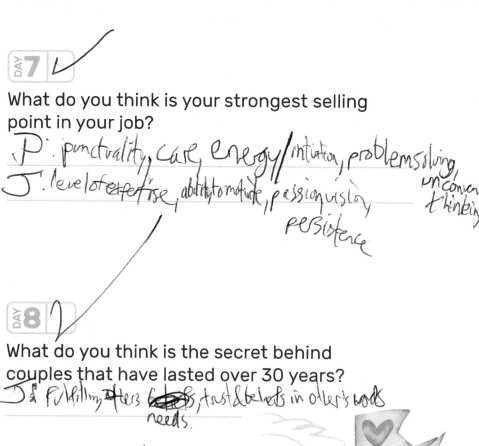

Do you tend to ask for help when you need it? Or do you usually suffer in silence?

DAY 10

Who would you choose as a dinner guest if you could invite anyone in the world?

_____

_____

 DAY 11

What hidden talent do you have that would surprise your partner?

_____

_____

DAY 12

If you could send a letter back through time to your younger self, what would it say?

_____

_____

DAY 13

What have you positively
changed the most since you
met your partner?

_____

_____

 DAY 14

Do you like to dance? What's your best move?
(bonus points if you break it out right now)

_____

_____

 DAY 15

Do you set high expectations for the people
in your life? Do they usually reach your
expectations?

_____

_____

DAY 16

What are five words that describe what you like most about your mate?

_____

_____

DAY 17

What was your favorite family vacation? Why was it so great?

_____

_____

DAY 18

What's the greatest personal challenge you've faced? How did it change your life?

_____

_____

19

What was your very first car? Did you buy it yourself or have it handed down to you?

_____

_____

 20

If you could be a pro at any sport, what would it be?

_____

_____

 21

What's something that you constantly worry about? Is it something your partner can ease your mind about?

_____

_____

22

What's your all-time favorite restaurant?

_____

_____

What's your biggest fear?

_____

_____

Do you like role-playing in bed? What's your favorite scenario?

_____

_____

Do you enjoy "me time"? How often?

_____

_____

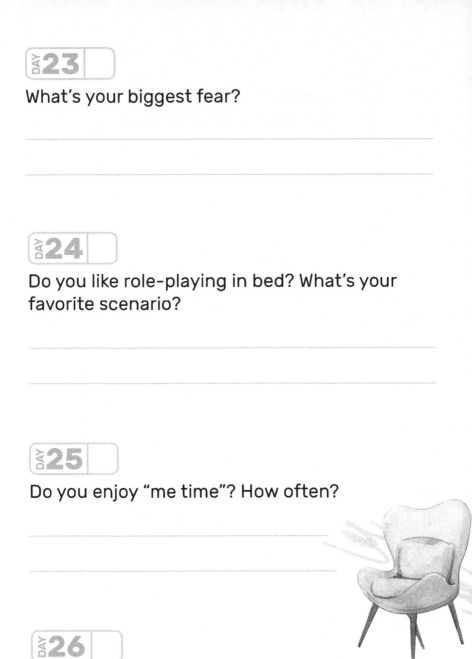

When do you feel like you're totally at peace?

_____

_____

DAY 27

Are you the kind of person that openly shares your opinion? Or do you wait until asked for it?

_____

_____

DAY 28

Have you ever embarrassed yourself at a social work function?

_____

_____

DAY 29

When was the last time you cried? Why?

_____

_____

DAY 30

What's one thing you can't say no to?

_____

_____

congrats!

You just finished your first month of couples Q & A!

Are you feeling more connected to each other?

Are you having fun finding out things you never knew about your partner?

Great! Then keep sharing your hopes, your dreams, and your crazy stories.

How competitive are you?
Give your best example.

Do you think you get embarrassed easily?

Besides your partner, who do you think knows
you better than anyone?

Have you ever cheated on a test?
Did you feel guilty about it?

 **35**

If you could choose the sex of your unborn child, what would it be?

_____

_____

 **36**

How often do you compliment people?

_____

_____

 **37**

Besides crying, how can someone tell if you're sad?

_____

_____

38

How do you distinguish between a friend and an acquaintance?

_____

_____

 **39**

Do you enjoy your own company? Or do you prefer to be around people most of the time?

 40

Do you feel like you make a difference with your job?

 **41**

What makes you feel inferior?

 **42**

Would you enjoy being famous? If so, how famous?

DAY 43

How many hours of sleep do you need per night?

_____

_____

DAY 44

Do you ever practice what you're going to say before making a phone call? Why?

_____

_____

DAY 45

Do you prefer to be the passenger or the driver?

_____

_____

DAY 46

If you were stranded on a desert island and could only bring three things, what would they be?

_____

_____

DAY 47

What's your favorite quote from a movie?

DAY 48

What motivates you the most?

DAY 49

How do you feel about people who gossip? Are you the kind of person that ignores them, or joins in?

DAY 50

How superstitious are you? What's the most superstitious thing that you've ever done?

 **51**

What's the most common factor amongst your friends?

 52

What's your favorite fast food joint? How often would you eat there if you didn't have to worry about your health?

53

Do you regularly set goals for yourself? What was the last time you achieved a goal you were proud of?

54

Which one of your friends makes you laugh the hardest, and why?

DAY 55

What's your favorite place to be alone?

_____

_____

DAY 56

In what setting are you most comfortable?

_____

_____

DAY 57

Do you like to cuddle after sex?
If so, for how long?

_____

_____

DAY 58

What's the biggest lie you've ever told a friend?

_____

_____

 **59**

What's the nicest thing a friend has done for you?

 60

What scent is nostalgic for you? Is it a good memory, or a bad one?

 **61**

On your list of a life's priorities, where does your career fall?

62

What would you consider to be a perfect day?

What do you think is the best invention in your lifetime?

_____

_____

How patient are you with people?
Give an example?

_____

_____

Did you ever attend a high school or college reunion? How did it go?

_____

_____

Do you consider yourself an organized person? Why?

_____

_____

DAY 67

What would make you give up your trust in a friend?

DAY 68

What's your most sensitive body part?

DAY 69

Do you think you're a gullible person? When has someone taken advantage of your trusting nature?

DAY 70

What family traditions do you want to carry on?

Do you believe in ghosts?
Have you ever seen one?

What's your all-time favorite TV show?

What's your favorite song?
How does it make you feel?

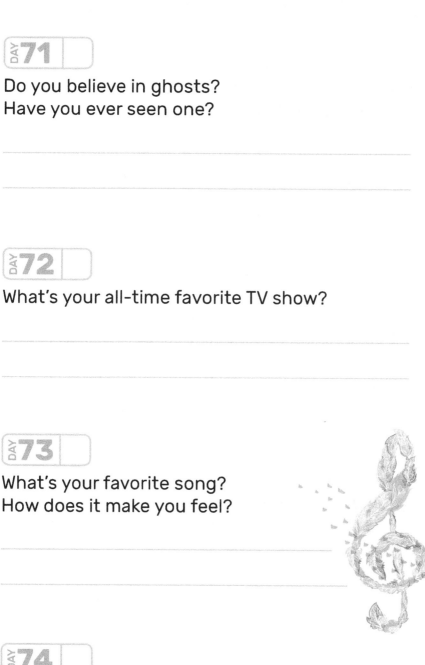

What makes your job worth getting up for?

DAY 75

Do you believe your horoscope sign describes your personality well?

_____

_____

DAY 76

Would you ever go to a nude beach and get fully nude?

_____

DAY 77

If you hit a car but nobody saw you and you would totally get away with it, would you leave a note? Or just leave?

_____

_____

DAY 78

Have you ever had to sacrifice your morals or ethics in a work situation?

_____

_____

DAY 79

What did you want to be when you
were younger?

_____

_____

DAY 80

Do you think you peaked in high school? Or
college? Or are you still on your way up and
have yet to peak?

_____

_____

DAY 81

When was the last time you sang to yourself or
to someone else?

_____

_____

DAY 82

What's your favorite cologne or perfume?

_____

_____

83

In recent years, what has been your favorite daydream?

84

Do you think our country will be better or worse in ten years?

85

If you were able to live to 100 and keep either the mind OR body of a 30-year-old for the last 70 years of your life, which would you choose?

86

What effect does stress have on you? How do you tend to deal with it?

What TV family would you compare your family to?

What was the worst dream you've ever had, and how do you interpret it?

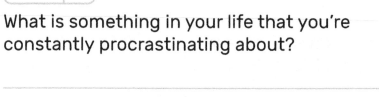

Do you have a secret intuition about how you will die?

What is something in your life that you're constantly procrastinating about?

DAY 91

Do you believe in extraterrestrials?
Have you ever seen a UFO?

DAY 92

If you could live one year of your life all over
again, what year would you choose?

DAY 93

In what ways does your job make you
feel proud?

DAY 94

Which of your friends have you known the
longest, and why have you been able to stay
such good friends?

Are you planning to donate your organs when you pass away? Why or why not?

What have you always wanted to do, but held back because of fear?

If the world was going to end in 10 minutes, what would be your last words to your partner?

Do you consider yourself a hard worker? Give an example.

DAY 99

Does your partner do anything that embarrasses you?

_____

_____

DAY 100

What one quality do you possess that makes you feel really special?

_____

_____

DAY 101

What's the biggest prank you've ever played on someone?

_____

_____

DAY 102

Name four things that you and your partner have in common.

_____

_____

What are you most thankful for in your life?

What's your greatest fear?

What is one thing you won't leave home without?

Have you ever been in a physical fight? How did it start?

DAY 107

What's your ideal number of times to have sex a week?

_____

_____

DAY 108

What would you alter about the way you were raised if you had the chance?

_____

_____

DAY 109

How did your parents discipline you? Would you discipline your children the same way?

_____

_____

DAY 110

What's your greatest personal strength? How has it helped your life?

_____

_____

DAY 111

Who did you tend to like more when you were growing up, your mom or your dad?

_____

_____

DAY 112

If you could write your own eulogy, what would it be?

_____

_____

DAY 113

What's your favorite movie of all time?

_____

_____

DAY 114

What are your top two pet peeves?

_____

_____

DAY 115

If you could change just one thing about your family, what would it be?

DAY 116

Take just three minutes and tell your partner as much about your life as you can.

DAY 117

Describe your most memorable birthday.

DAY 118

Do you tend to exaggerate things?

DAY 119

What was your most memorable
childhood experience?

DAY 120

What are your favorite props to have fun
with in bed?

DAY 121

Have you ever been hospitalized?

DAY 122

What's the most spontaneous thing
you've ever done?

DAY 123

If you could gain any one quality or ability, what would it be?

_____

_____

DAY 124

Who do you model yourself after professionally, and what about them do you admire?

_____

_____

DAY 125

What would you want to know if a crystal ball could tell you the truth about your life, and the future?

_____

_____

DAY 126

What do you love most about your current job?

_____

_____

 **127**

What personal quality would you most like to improve?

 128

What was your worst family vacation? Why was it so bad?

129

Do you screen phone calls before answering?

130

What's the biggest fight you've ever had with your family?

DAY 131

Is there something you've been wanting to do for a long time? Why haven't you gone ahead and done it?

DAY 132

When was the last time you gave a speech? Were you nervous?

DAY 133

What do you think is the best accomplishment of your whole life?

DAY 134

What are the three words that you would use to describe yourself? Can you give me an example of how you possess each?

What was the first concert you've ever been to? Do you still like that band?

_____

_____

What qualities do you look for in a friend?

_____

_____

What's the nicest thing that a stranger has ever done for you?

_____

_____

Have you ever lost someone very special to you? What effect did it have on you?

_____

_____

DAY 139

If you were to mentor someone, what words of wisdom would you give them?

_____

_____

DAY 140

What was your first impression of your partner? How has it changed over time?

_____

_____

DAY 141

Who's the most famous person you've ever met?

_____

_____

DAY 142

How often do you pray? Do you consider yourself a very religious person?

_____

_____

DAY 143

Do you think you're paid what you're worth
at your job?

DAY 144

What makes you feel sexy?

DAY 145

What is the most cherished memory you have?

DAY 146

Are you more similar to your mom or your dad?

DAY 147

Five years ago, did you picture yourself in the life you are currently in?

_____

_____

DAY 148

Do you consider yourself a lucky person? How much of life do you think depends on luck?

_____

_____

DAY 149

What's your greatest insecurity?

_____

_____

DAY 150

What are your career goals in the next few years?

_____

_____

 **151**

What's your favorite season, and why?

 152

What is your ideal vacation if money was no object?

 153

What do you think makes the biggest difference between a good parent and a great parent?

 154

Do you think you can identify people that are in love? What do you look for?

 **155**

In general, do you tend to blame others for your problems?

 156

What's the greatest career challenge you've faced?

 **157**

What is your most dreadful recollection?

 158

What was your first job and how much were you paid?

Who do you get along with best in your extended family?

_____

_____

Would you alter anything about the way you live now if you knew you would die abruptly in a year?

_____

_____

Do you prefer your work superiors to be the same sex as you?

_____

_____

If you could be anyone in the world for 24 hours, who would it be?

_____

_____

DAY 163

Do you want your partner to tell you when you haven't been sexually satisfied in bed?

_____

_____

DAY 164

Did you ever run away from home as a child? Where did you go?

_____

_____

DAY 165

What's the nicest thing you've ever done for a stranger?

_____

_____

DAY 166

What do you think your family is most proud of you for?

_____

_____

 **167**

Did you ever hang out with the wrong crowd in high school?

 **168**

What celebrity do people say you look like? Do you agree?

 **169**

What's the craziest thing you've ever done on a dare?

 **170**

How do you know when you've had too much to drink?

DAY 171

What do you hate most about your current job?

_____

_____

DAY 172

Do you remember your first dance in school? Were you a wallflower or were you out on the dance floor on the first song?

_____

_____

DAY 173

What was the most significant turning point in your career?

_____

_____

DAY 174

What experience has given you an extreme adrenaline rush?

_____

_____

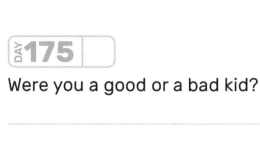

DAY 175

Were you a good or a bad kid?

_____

_____

DAY 176

Have you ever had a mentor? What was the most important thing they taught you?

_____

_____

DAY 177

What brings out the animal in you?

_____

_____

DAY 178

At what age did you hit puberty? Did you have any embarrassing experiences during it?

_____

_____

 **179**

Where was your favorite place to hang out when you were growing up?

_____

_____

 **180**

What place do you fantasize about having sex?

_____

_____

181

What were you teased about as a child? Do you think it had any permanent effect on you?

_____

_____

182

What are the qualities that you think would make you a good boss?

_____

_____

If you could have any magical power, what would it be?

When have you felt the proudest of yourself?

What was your favorite family pet when you were growing up?

If your partner became your "sex slave for a day" what would you make them do?

DAY 187

What does a good friendship mean to you?

_____

_____

DAY 188

In general, do you think you have a positive outlook on life?

_____

_____

DAY 189

How would your closest friend describe you?

_____

_____

DAY 190

How many different types of love do you think there are?

_____

_____

Are you a punctual person or always late?

Do you think you succeeded with most of the goals that you set in high school?

If you could be any animal for 24 hours, what would you be?

Have you ever faked an orgasm?

 **195**

Go back and forth and share 3 things that you think are good characteristics of your partner.

_____

_____

 **196**

How would you describe your ideal boss?

_____

_____

197

What's the dumbest thing you've ever done while drinking?

_____

_____

198

What situations have you been able to talk your way out of?

_____

_____

Do you think you're sexy when you're naked?

_____

_____

Did you ever get grounded as a kid? What were you usually in trouble for?

_____

_____

Is your family close and welcoming? Do you believe you had a happier childhood than the majority of people?

_____

_____

What's your favorite fantasy in bed?

_____

_____

What brings about your temper?

_____

_____

Who was your favorite babysitter? What about them did you like?

_____

_____

If you could be the best at anything in the world, what would it be?

_____

_____

Do you sing in the shower? Do you think your partner thinks you have a good voice?

_____

_____

What was your nickname in school? Did your family have a nickname for you?

What was the best advice you've given to a friend?

Are you stubborn? Give an example.

On a scale of 1-10, how dirty is your mind?

What do you think is your most bizarre fetish?

_____

_____

What was your last erotic dream about?

_____

_____

What did you hate about high school?
And what did you love about it?

_____

_____

When have you felt the most disappointed
in yourself?

_____

_____

 **215**

How would your parents describe what it was like raising you? What do you think they had the most challenge with?

 **216**

What were your favorite toys to play with as a kid?

 **217**

What was the first thing you liked about your partner?

218

How many times have you had your heart broken?

Besides your partner, what's the first thing you think about when you wake up?

_____

_____

Have you ever stolen anything?
How old were you?

_____

_____

Do you work well under pressure?

_____

_____

How do you feel about your emotional connection with your mother?

_____

_____

DAY 223

Have you ever spied on someone?
Did you get caught?

_____

_____

DAY 224

How would you describe your closest friends?

_____

_____

DAY 225

What fantasy of yours is most embarrassing?

_____

_____

DAY 226

Do you plan ahead or take life one day
at a time?

_____

_____

DAY 227

If you could choose your cause of death, what would it be?

_____

_____

DAY 228

What is one of your favorite guilty pleasures?

_____

_____

DAY 229

Did you have an opportunity to know your grandparents? What was the best lesson you learned from them?

_____

_____

DAY 230

Do you keep any secrets from your family?

_____

_____

DAY 231

What's one mistake you've made that you would like to forget?

DAY 232

Were you bullied when you were growing up? Or were you the bully?

DAY 233

What do you wish your partner would do more of in bed?

DAY 234

If you could travel back to the past, what time period would you want to go?

DAY 235

On a scale of 1 to 10, how strong do you think your sex drive is?

DAY 236

Are you good at do-it-yourself projects?

DAY 237

Have you ever mooned anyone?

DAY 238

How many times a day do you think about sex?

 **239**

What was your favorite place to travel outside of your country?

 **240**

What is your definition of love?

 **241**

When have you felt the proudest of yourself?

242

In your relationship priorities, where does sex rate?

 **243**

What's a childhood secret you've never told anyone about?

_____

_____

 **244**

Which of the Seven Dwarves do you most relate to?

_____

_____

 **245**

If you were granted the true answer to any question in the world, what would you ask?

_____

_____

 **246**

How good are you at keeping secrets? What's a secret you regret sharing?

_____

_____

DAY 247

Did you have an imaginary friend growing up? How would you describe them?

DAY 248

How often did your family move when you were younger?

DAY 249

Did you go to your prom? Was it a positive or negative experience?

DAY 250

What's your favorite way to celebrate good news?

DAY 251

What was your favorite game to play when you were growing up?

_____

_____

DAY 252

What lessons have you learned the hard way?

_____

_____

DAY 253

What's the worst date you've ever had?

_____

_____

DAY 254

What was your favorite Halloween costume ever?

_____

_____

 **255**

If friends from high school could see you now, what do you think their impression would be?

 256

What do you think is the greatest difference between you and your partner?
What's the greatest similarity?

257

Have you ever had a near-death experience?

258

What's the last book you read?
What did you like about it?

DAY 259

Besides your partner, what person has had the greatest positive impact on your life?

_____

_____

DAY 260

Do you tend to focus more on the past, present, or future?

_____

_____

DAY 261

How good are you at remembering important dates?

_____

_____

DAY 262

Tell your partner what you admire about them, stating things you wouldn't say to a stranger.

_____

_____

DAY 263

What was your scariest experience?

DAY 264

What's your idea of "roughing it"?

DAY 265

What kind of grades did you get in high school? Do you think it reflected on your intelligence?

DAY 266

Which of your personality traits do you attribute to your mom? Which traits do you get from your dad?

Have you ever been skinny dipping?

If you could master any musical instrument, what would it be?

Who was your first best friend growing up? How long did that relationship last?

How do you think you could be a better friend to your current group of friends?

271

What do you remember about your first day
of Kindergarten?

_____

_____

272

Tell your partner about an embarrassing
moment in your life.

_____

_____

273

Who taught you about the "birds and the bees?"
Was it an awkward conversation?

_____

_____

274

How often do you like to get dressed
up for a night out on the town?

_____

_____

DAY 275

When was the last time you cried in front of another person?
When was the last time you cried by yourself?

DAY 276

Who's your idol? Do you model your life after them?

DAY 277

Did you ever sneak out of your house when you were in high school? Did you ever get caught?

DAY 278

How often do you take risks? What's the biggest risk you've taken lately?

 **279**

What's your favorite love song?
(bonus points if you sing it!)

_____

_____

 **280**

Have you ever had a DNA test to find out your
ancestry? What was most surprising about it?

_____

_____

 **281**

Tell your partner something you already admire
about them.

_____

_____

282

What's your favorite holiday?
Which is your least favorite?

_____

_____

Do you like striking up conversations with strangers? What's the best thing a stranger has ever said to you?

Do you shy away from cameras or welcome them?

What do you think is something that is too serious to be joked about?

What's your favorite outfit?
How does it make you feel?

DAY 287

What's your biggest pet peeve?

DAY 288

How often do you overdraft your checking account?

DAY 289

When arguing, do you prefer to be the one to walk away, or do you stay in the argument until you've had the final word?

DAY 290

If you could be any cartoon character, who would you choose to be?

What is a good habit that you wish you could pick up?

_____

_____

Do you consider yourself a vengeful person? Who would you get even with if there were no repercussions?

_____

_____

When was the last time you went out of your way to make someone feel really special?

_____

_____

What was your neighborhood like when you were growing up?

_____

_____

295

Do you consider yourself a leader or a follower?

296

What was your most memorable family car?

297

What's the best thing about being in love?

298

What's the best way that you've found to help you cope with being sad?

 **299**

How do you think you act when you're angry?
How about when you're happy?

_____

_____

 **300**

Do you prefer to make the first move or have it
be made on you?

_____

_____

 **301**

What's the most romantic gift you think you
could ever receive?

_____

_____

302

What would you most regret not telling
someone if you died tonight?

_____

_____

 **303**

How good is your sense of direction?

 **304**

If your wardrobe could only be one color, what would it be?

 **305**

Do you fear death? If you could choose, how would you prefer to pass away?

306

Do you think you act your age?

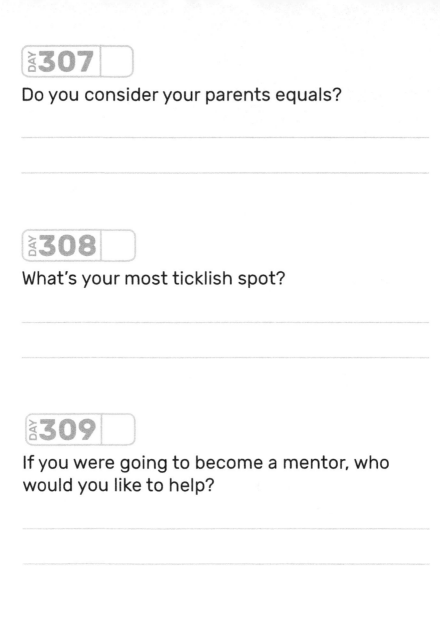

DAY 307

Do you consider your parents equals?

DAY 308

What's your most ticklish spot?

DAY 309

If you were going to become a mentor, who would you like to help?

DAY 310

What do you think is the best asset you bring into a relationship?

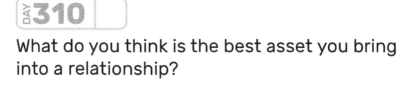

Have you ever been stalked by an ex?

What's the best lesson you've learned from a bad past relationship?

What's your favorite way to pamper yourself?

How would you describe your dream honeymoon?

DAY 315

How would you describe your ideal
dream house?

_____

_____

DAY 316

Do you consider yourself spiritual?

_____

_____

DAY 317

If you and your partner were strangers and met
at a bar, how would you want your partner to hit
on you?

_____

_____

DAY 318

Is compromise hard for you? Why or why not?

_____

_____

Do you think it's harder to be a man or a woman these days?

How do you feel when your partner talks about past relationships?

Which character in Star Wars are you most like?

What one quality in your partner do you appreciate the most?

DAY 323

How do you define happiness?

_____

_____

DAY 324

If you could change one of your physical features, what would it be?

_____

_____

DAY 325

What do you think is the sexiest style of underwear on your partner?

_____

_____

DAY 326

What brings out the child in you?

_____

_____

DAY 327

If you could do something totally out of character but remain anonymous, what would you do?

_____

_____

DAY 328

Would you want your children to grow up just like you? Why?

_____

_____

DAY 329

What was your favorite subject in grade school?

_____

DAY 330

If you could have a vacation home in any part of the world, where would it be?

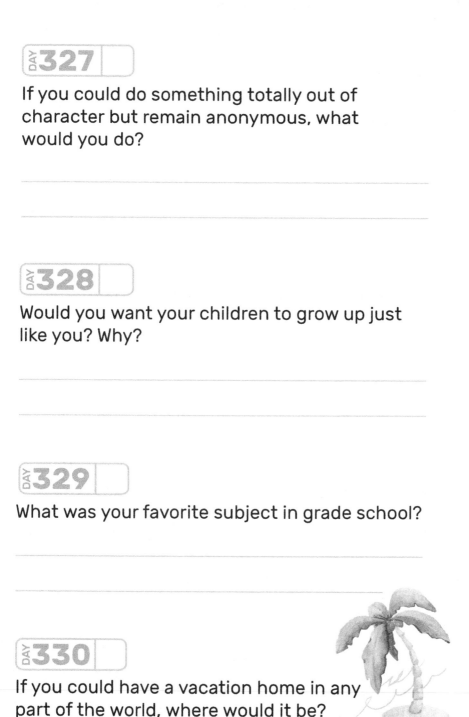

_____

_____

DAY 331

What do you think is the most romantic kind of food to cook for your partner?

_____

_____

DAY 332

What was your favorite cereal growing up?

_____

_____

DAY 333

Do you believe people can change? What's the biggest change you've seen in yourself in the past 10 years?

_____

_____

DAY 334

Besides your partner, who would you die for without thinking twice?

_____

_____

If you could describe your life with the title of a song, what would it be?

After saving your loved ones and pets from a house fire, you have time to make a final run to save only one item. What would you save, and why?

Are you a jealous person?
What makes you most jealous in a relationship?

What's the most embarrassing thing you have in your bedroom drawer or closet?

DAY 339

Besides your partner, who's your favorite person to turn to when you're sad or upset?

DAY 340

Have you ever talked your way out of a ticket? What were you doing wrong?

DAY 341

If someone has their zipper down, do you tell them right away?

DAY 342

What do you think would be your partner's biggest complaint about you?

How would you describe your driving style?

_____

_____

What's your opinion about capital punishment?

_____

_____

How often do you look in the mirror? Do
you think you could go a whole day without
looking in one?

_____

_____

Do your religious beliefs influence your
everyday decisions?

_____

_____

347

What do you think is the most important thing in a relationship?

348

What was your first impression upon meeting your partner? Has that impression changed over time?

349

Whose death in your family would you find most upsetting, and why?

350

What are your parents' occupations? Did their work influence what you do for a living?

DAY 351

Would you rather cook, or be cooked for?

_____

_____

DAY 352

Which traffic law do you disobey most often?

_____

_____

DAY 353

If your partner has a trait that annoys you, what do you think is the best way to bring it up?

_____

_____

DAY 354

If you could live your life in a movie, what movie would it be, and what character would you play?

_____

_____

DAY 355

What's your favorite breakfast food?

DAY 356

What's the least romantic
gift you've ever received?

DAY 357

Do you consider yourself a good listener?
How do you think you could improve?

DAY 358

Share a personal problem with your partner and
seek their opinion on how to address it.

 **359**

What's your ideal job if money wasn't a factor?

 **360**

Do you consider yourself a morning person or a night person?

 **361**

Where's your favorite place to relax?

 **362**

Have you ever been arrested and spent the night in jail?

 **363**

What personal belief do you feel so strongly about that you'll never compromise?

 **364**

Do you think men and women can just be friends?

 **365**

How do you define intimacy?

Made in United States
Orlando, FL
11 December 2023

40636561R00055